HOLIDAYS & HEROES

Let's Celebrate

THANKSGIVING DAY

BY Barbara deRubertis

ILLUSTRATED BY Thomas Sperling

THE WAMPANOAG AND THE PILGRIMS

The Kane Press • New York

For activities and resources for this book and others in the HOLIDAYS & HEROES series, visit: www.kanepress.com/holidays-and-heroes

Text copyright © 1992 by The Kane Press
Original illustrations on pages 1, 4, 7, 8, 9, 10, 11, 14, 15, 16, 18, 21, 22, 25, 27, 28, 32 copyright © 1992 by The Kane Press
Photograph/image copyrights: cover © Library of Congress, LC-USZC4-4961; page 3 © Angela Waye/ Shutterstock; 4 © Library of Congress, Detroit Publishing Company Collection, LC-D419-14; 5 © Library of Congress, LC-USZC4-4311; 6 © Library of Congress, Currier & Ives, LC-USZ62-3461; 10 © Courtesy of Pilgrim Hall Museum, Plymouth MA; 12 © Associated Press; 13 © Getty Images; 17 © Library of Congress, LC-USZ62-96230; 18 © Marilyn Barbone/Shutterstock; 19 © Associated Press; 20 © Tomas Pavelka/Shutterstock; 23 © Library of Congress, LC-USZ62-3030; 24 © Unholy Vault Designs/Shutterstock; 26 © Library of Congress, LC-USZ62-96220/Florida Center for Instructional Technology; 29: clams © Jiang Hongyan/Shutterstock, squash © An Nguyen/Shutterstock, mussel © O.Bellini/Shutterstock, chestnuts © Hellen Grig/Shutterstock, cranberries © Lisovskaya Natalia/ Shutterstock, beans © Jeehyun/Shutterstock, corn © Svanblar/Shutterstock, pumpkin © Jacek Fulawka/ Shutterstock; 30–31 © Library of Congress, LC-USZC4-4961
All due diligence has been conducted in identifying copyright holders and obtaining permissions.

Library of Congress Cataloging-in-Publication Data

deRubertis, Barbara.
  Let's Celebrate Thanksgiving Day / by Barbara deRubertis ; illustrated by Thomas Sperling. — Revised Edition.
    pages cm. — (Holidays & heroes)
  ISBN 978-1-57565-636-6 (pbk. : alk. paper) — ISBN 978-1-57565-637-3 (e-book)
  1. Thanksgiving Day—Juvenile literature. I. Sperling, Thomas, 1952- illustrator. II. Title.
  GT4975.D47 2013
  394.2649—dc23
                              2013001585

Library reinforced binding ISBN: 978-1-57565-723-3

1 3 5 7 9 10 8 6 4 2

Revised edition first published in the United States of America in 2013 by Kane Press, Inc.
Printed in the United States of America

Book Design: Edward Miller
Photograph/Image Research: Maura Taboubi

Visit us online at **www.kanepress.com.**

 Like us on Facebook
facebook.com/kanepress

 Follow us on Twitter
@KanePress

Pronunciation Guide

Massasoit = MASS-uh-soyt
Wampanoag = WOM-puh-NO-ag
Sachem = SATCH-um
Plimoth (old spelling) = PLIM-uth
Plymouth (present-day spelling) = PLIM-uth
Patuxet = Puh-TUX-ut
Samoset = SAM-oh-set
Squanto (Tisquantum) = SKWAN-toe

Massasoit was Chief of the Wampanoag. Each Wampanoag village had a leader called a "sachem." But Massasoit was Chief Sachem of all the villages.

He was a wise and powerful leader.

Massasoit must have been worried when he heard that about a hundred English settlers had come to his land!

It was **November of 1620** when these settlers first arrived on a ship called the *Mayflower*. The ship dropped anchor off the coast of land that is now part of the state of Massachusetts.

Some of the people onboard the ship were called "Pilgrims." They had come to this land to find freedom. Others who traveled with them were also hoping to find a better life.

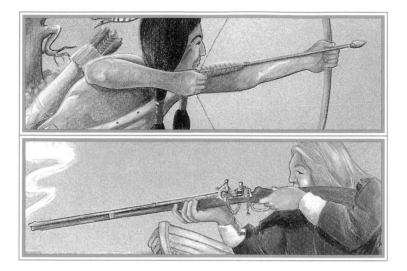

For weeks the Pilgrims searched for a good place to settle. One time, arrows were shot at them. They fired back with their muskets.

No one was hurt. But everyone was worried. The Wampanoag were worried about these English settlers. The English were worried about the people they called "Indians."

Finally, the Pilgrims found a good harbor at the place named "Plimoth" on their map.

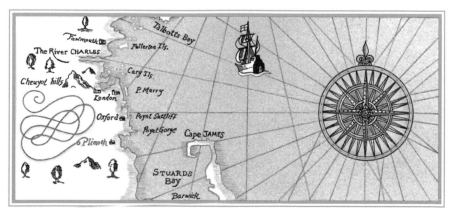

A map of the Massachusetts coast as described by the early explorer John Smith

After November came **December.**
The season of WINTER began.

*Winter at Plymouth was black
  and white.
It was dark and damp and cold.
The gray of hunger and sickness
  arrived,
and tales of sadness were told.*

At Plymouth, the Pilgrims found land that had already been cleared. They did not know that the land had once been a Wampanoag village called Patuxet.

The settlers continued to live on the *Mayflower* while they built a Common House. It would be used as a storehouse and as a church.

After December came
January and **February**.

The Indians must have
wondered how the settlers could
possibly survive the winter.
They had arrived too late to
plant crops. They did not have
time to build warm houses.
In the coldest days of winter,
the settlers almost ran out
of food. Most of them
suffered from terrible
sickness. Only six or
seven people remained
healthy. They were kept
busy taking care of all the
others.
The Common House
was used as a hospital.

Before the sickness was over, almost half of the settlers died.

William Bradford

Later, a Pilgrim named William Bradford wrote about this time. He said that those who took care of the sick showed true love for their friends.

If the Wampanoag watched the settlers, they watched silently, from a distance.

Chief Massasoit knew how terrible sickness could be. Sometimes entire Wampanoag villages had been wiped out because of sickness.

Would any of these new settlers survive?

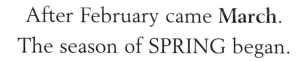

After February came **March**.
The season of SPRING began.

Spring was painted a soft, new green
for the colorful flowers earth sends.
The season of hope arrived at last.
It came in the shape of friends.

In March, the first Indian visitor walked into Plymouth. His name was Samoset. Samoset surprised the settlers by greeting them in English!

On his third visit, Samoset brought a Wampanoag friend named Squanto, who spoke even better English.

Many years before, Squanto had been captured and taken to England. There he had learned to speak English. When he finally returned home to Patuxet, he learned that all the people of his village had died from a terrible sickness.

Squanto now told the settlers that Chief Massasoit himself was coming to visit them.

Left: Samoset visits the settlers.

Right: Squanto

Massasoit, the Chief Sachem of the
Wampanoag, came with sixty of his people!
He had decided to make peace.

These settlers were weak, but they had
powerful weapons. The settlers could
help his people.

And he could help the settlers.

Massasoit looked splendid. The mulberry red
paint on his face showed he was an important
leader.

He wore a turkey feather in his hair.
Around his neck hung beads of white bone.
His coat, leggings, and moccasins
were made of animal skins.

With a ceremony fit for a king, the settlers welcomed Massasoit. He was presented with gifts of knives, jewelry, and food.

Then he was led to an unfinished house. Quickly, a rug and cushions were laid on the floor.

Drums rolled. Trumpets sounded. Six men saluted with their muskets. The Pilgrim leader, Governor John Carver, entered. He bowed to kiss Massasoit's hand. Massasoit then did the same.

Chief Massasoit and Governor Carver made a peace treaty that lasted more than fifty years! Sadly, some later European settlers were not as respectful of the Indians they met.

A Pilgrim later wrote that Massasoit was truly a great chief. He ruled by reason, not force. He always told the truth. And his word could be trusted.

Meeting of Massasoit and Governor Carver

After March came **April** and **May**.

Squanto decided to stay with
the settlers at Plymouth. He taught
them many things. He said that the time to plant
seed was when the oak leaves grew to the size of
a mouse's ear.

He showed the settlers how to plant Indian
corn. Fish, he said, should be planted with the
seed! The fish would help the corn grow tall and
strong.

Beans could also be planted in the same hole.
Their vines would climb up the corn stalks. And
pumpkins could grow on the ground below.

The Wampanoag called corn, beans, and
squash "The Three Sisters."

During that spring of peace and hope, a sad event also happened. Governor Carver died. The settlers chose William Bradford as their new governor.

The people of Plymouth must have thought he was a good governor. They elected him thirty more times!

Statue of William Bradford in Plymouth, Massachusetts

After May came **June**, **July**, and **August**.
The season of SUMMER had arrived.

*Summer brought Plymouth skies of blue
lit by a yellow sun.
The children picked bright red berries
    and plums
when the long day's work was done.*

Squanto also taught the settlers other things.

To catch fish.

To hunt deer with bow and arrow.

To dig clams and eels out of the mud.

To tap maple trees for sap to make syrup and sugar.

To know which plants were food, which were poison, and which were medicine.

The settlers worked in their fields.

They finished seven houses built with pine boards and thatched roofs. They made beds, benches, stools, and tables. They dipped candles and made soap.

The children worked just as hard as their parents.

But on Sundays, the Pilgrims neither
worked nor played. They went to church.

After August came **September** and **October**.
It was now the season of AUTUMN.

Autumn was russet and golden and brown,
like the ripening fields of corn.
The Indians and settlers were helping each other,
and a shared Thanksgiving was born.

Finally, the last of the harvest was brought in. The seed brought from England had done poorly. But the Indian corn harvest was excellent. The settlers would have plenty of food for the coming winter.

Governor Bradford decided it was a good time for a celebration. They would have a Thanksgiving festival at Plymouth!

Chief Massasoit, of course, would be invited. The settlers were very grateful to him and all the Wampanoag people.

Chief Massasoit

Chief Massasoit certainly would have understood why the settlers wanted to have a Thanksgiving festival. The Wampanoag also had festivals to give thanks for a good harvest.

During their harvest festivals, the Wampanoag feasted, danced, held contests, and played games. They also gave part of what they had to the poor. And they gave something back to the earth.

They believed that people cannot just *take* without *giving*.

Preparation for the Thanksgiving feast took many days. The men went hunting for geese, ducks, and turkeys. These would be roasted over open fires.

The four married women who had survived the winter did all the cooking. It was a big job! Of course, the children helped.

clams

cranberries

acorn squash

mussel

chestnuts

kidney beans

Berries and nuts were gathered, and corn was used to make bread. Fish and shellfish were smoked, dried, or simmered in thick, steaming soup.

Pumpkin was probably cooked over hot coals or stewed—but not baked in pies.

corn

pumpkin

Chief Massasoit arrived for Thanksgiving at Plymouth with ninety of his people! Fortunately, they also brought five deer as a gift. There were nearly 150 people to feed!

Everyone enjoyed feasting on the delicious food. Then they put on shows for each other. The settlers marched and fired their weapons. The Indians showed their skill with bows and arrows.

They also held contests and played games. The Indians and Pilgrims were surprised to discover that many of their games were similar!

Everyone was having such a good time that the festival lasted for three days.

Today, almost four hundred years later, we remember that festival when we celebrate Thanksgiving Day.

A year, with twelve months and four seasons, had passed for the settlers at Plymouth.

The Indians and Pilgrims were different, it's true.
They also were much the same!
With talking and sharing, with helping and caring,
first peace, then friendship, came.

Chief Massasoit probably wondered what the future would hold. But for now, the Wampanoag and the Pilgrims had made peace, and they were friends.